Cornerstones of Freedom

The Mississippi Flood of 1993

Karin Luisa Badt

CHILDRENS PRESS®
CHICAGO

Library of Congress Cataloging-in-Publication Data

Badt, Karin Luisa.
  Mississippi Flood of 1993 / by Karin Luisa Badt.
    p. cm. - (Cornerstones of freedom)
  ISBN 0-516-06680-3
  1. Floods—Mississippi River Valley—History—20th
century—Juvenile literature. 2. Mississippi River Valley—
History—1865– —Juvenile literature. I. Title. II. Series.
F355.B33 1994
977'.033 – dc20   94-9493
                                                      CIP
                                                      AC

When fifteen-year-old Amy Robinson went to sleep on the night of July 22, 1993, she listened to the familiar sound of rain. She had grown used to rain and thunder. It had been raining every day for three months in St. Charles, Missouri.

At two in the morning, Amy's mother was in her room, shaking her awake. Her mother's face was white, her eyes lit with fear as she told Amy to get dressed immediately. As she got out of bed, Amy's feet stretched to the floor, but they did not touch the familiar warm rug that lay next to her bed. Instead, her feet plunged into icy cold water! The Mississippi River was bubbling through the floor. Through the window, Amy could no longer see the front yard. Everything

was water. Her house had become an island.

Amy and her family evacuated their home and spent the summer of 1993 in motel rooms and shelters. They were not alone. Tens of thousands of families in nine states across the Midwest were forced to abandon their homes that summer. The Mississippi River and its tributaries (the smaller rivers that flow into a large river) were swollen from months of rain. The water eventually broke loose and flooded acres of land, claiming lives, destroying neighborhoods, ruining homes.

The poet T. S. Eliot described the Mississippi River as "a strong brown god—sullen, untamed and intractable." The Ojibwa Indians named it the "Father of the Waters." Starting as a small stream in Minnesota, the mighty Mississippi

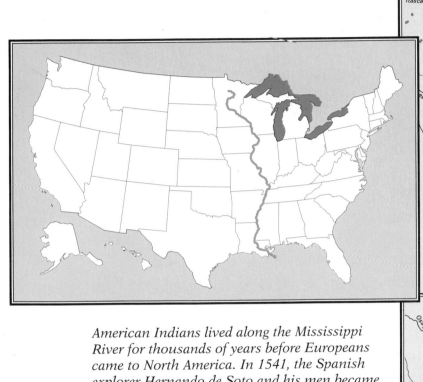

American Indians lived along the Mississippi River for thousands of years before Europeans came to North America. In 1541, the Spanish explorer Hernando de Soto and his men became the first Europeans to see the Mississippi. In 1682, another explorer, Robert La Salle, claimed the river for France. The United States eventually bought the Mississippi from France in 1803 as part of the Louisiana Purchase. In the years before the railroad industry was established, the Mississippi was the most important trade route in the United States.

Fast Facts About the Mississippi River

Source: Lake Itasca, Minnesota

Outflow: Gulf of Mexico

Length: 2,340 miles (3,776 kilometers)

Deepest point: 100 feet (30 meters)

Shallowest point: 9 feet (2.7 meters)

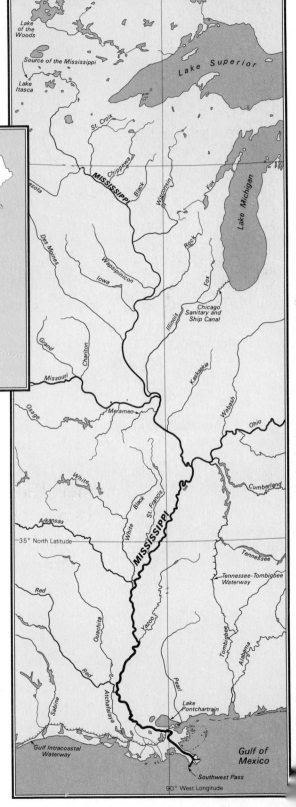

Tents that housed victims of the 1927 Mississippi flood

winds through the American Midwest to the Gulf of Mexico, growing bigger as it flows south. It collects the waters of many other rivers, such as the Ohio, the Missouri, and the Illinois.

The Mississippi is a glorious river, a marvel of nature. But it can also be a dangerous river. It naturally overflows every year during the rainy season. And almost every decade, it creates floods. In the twentieth century alone, there have been tremendous Mississippi floods in 1927, 1937, 1965, and 1973. After the great flood of 1927, the federal government arranged to

Top: Prisoners patch a levee in the 1937 flood. Bottom: West Alton, Missouri, is engulfed by the Mississippi in 1973.

build levees and dams along the entire length of the river. A levee is a long wall of dirt built alongside a river to keep it from overflowing. The first levees were built four thousand years ago by the Egyptians alongside the Nile. They had to keep the water out in order for their country to survive.

The land right next to a river is called a floodplain because it is subject to periodic flooding. People on or near a floodplain know it is a dangerous place to live. They build their homes there despite the high risk of a flood roaring up and swallowing everything in sight. In fact, for many people on the Mississippi floodplains, the 1993 flood was not their first. So why do people continue choosing to live there?

One reason is that the farmland is excellent. The land around a river is extremely fertile. Every time a river floods its banks, it deposits silt—sediment that makes the soil rich with minerals. Crops grow wonderfully along the banks. Ancient Egypt could not have grown into a fabulous civilization if not for the rich soil around the Nile River.

Another important reason why people live on floodplains is that they have their roots there. Walter King, of Alexandria, Missouri, said, "It's our sense of home, see? Our families have been here forever. We're river people."

Many of the families who live along the Mississippi are descendants of the French, Irish, and German settlers who came in the 1800s to settle along the coast. They were attracted by the rich farmland. Other people, however, like to live near a river just because it is peaceful and beautiful. The water flows quietly under the trees, golden and mysterious under the sun. And some people can go fishing right from their own backyards.

But these people spent many anxious days in the summer of 1993, waiting to see if the levee protecting their town would hold back the flood, or let the water burst through. Once the

A levee in Monroe County, Illinois, bursts, and a farm is destroyed by the unstoppable rushing water.

To thousands of Midwesterners, the Mississippi River is both a friend and a powerful enemy.

water made a break, there was no stopping the flood from taking over. The brown, muddy water would sneak up and drown everything in its path.

The front pages of newspapers were filled with daily accounts of which levees were holding and which had burst. Sometimes the news was good. On Wednesday, July 28th, the headline of the *St. Louis Post Dispatch* joyfully announced: "Kansas City Levees Hold." Kansas City was saved—a major disaster had been averted.

Not every town was so lucky. Many towns along the Mississippi and its tributaries were defended by private levees, built by farmer

A St. Charles, Missouri, farmer looks out on what was once hundreds of acres of farmland.

cooperatives or municipalities. These levees were not as strong or high as the levees the federal government had built. Seventy percent of the 1,110 private levees broke under the force of the water.

When you imagine a river flood, you should not picture a great big tidal wave surging towards you at breakneck speed. A river flood moves slowly, no faster than a person can walk. "Every day it was a little closer," explained Vernon McClane, who saw the flood inch its way down the road toward his house in West Alton, Missouri. People knew the flood was coming weeks in advance.

Even though everyone was prepared for a flood, many people didn't leave their homes until the water was lapping at their doorstep. Nobody wants to abandon their home. What do you do without a home? Where do you go? While some people could stay with family, many more had to go to a shelter or a motel, and some just slept in their cars.

A few people refused to leave their homes. Some people chose to live in the second story of their house. They would get in and out of the house by climbing through a second-floor window.

Gary Iffrig couldn't bear to leave the farm where his family had lived for six generations. He wouldn't let the flood kick him off his property. After his farmhouse went underwater, he camped

Some people find it impossible to abandon their homes, even when floodwater creeps up their front yard . . . and higher.

out in a tent for more than a month, fighting off snakes and "spiders as big as your fist."

Some people had to fight for their lives. Harold Smith was in his pickup truck when he thought he heard a break in the Mississippi levee near his home. The next moment, his truck was engulfed in ten feet of churning floodwater. He managed to swim out the window of his truck.

The family car becomes unusable in a flood, but getting around in a boat can be very dangerous.

Glen Grotegeers of West Alton, Missouri, was in his boat when a tree crashed, splitting the boat in two. Luckily, he was wearing his life jacket, because he went sprawling into the water. The current of the river grabbed him, and he was rushed downstream. He knew his only hope was to reach land, but how? He was in the middle of the Mississippi River! He managed to grab onto a tree still rooted in the ground. He climbed into the branches and spent the night there. In the morning, he found a wooden plank and used it as a kickboard. Down the river he went, resting every once in a while where he could find an "island" made by a submerged

14

This photograph, taken from a satellite orbiting the earth, shows the floodwater overflowing its banks at North Cape Girardeau, Missouri. Trees are shown in red; light blue dots are flooded buildings; and dark blue is river water.

shed. Finally, twenty miles and two days later, he pulled himself up onto a levee in St. Louis. "The life jacket saved me," he said.

The 1993 flood will go down in history as the most destructive ever in the United States. Fifty people died. Two hundred counties were declared disaster areas. More than 17,000 square miles of land were drenched in water. Some 40,000 houses were evacuated, and many more were hopelessly ruined. The floodwater smashed windows, ate up furniture, and soaked through walls. It turned busy downtown areas into swamps. What was once a store or a bank became a battered building submerged in water.

The flood even ripped up cemeteries, sending caskets floating down the river.

Entire villages disappeared from the map. In Hull, Illinois, a town of 513 people, virtually every home was flooded. Kaskaskia, Illinois, an old French settlement on an island, was completely underwater. You could only see the tips of rooftops, like icebergs sticking out of the ocean. The list of the dead towns grew as the summer rains continued to pour. In Illinois alone, the towns of Meyer, Niota, and Valmeyer were all swept away. The inhabitants of these and other towns not only lost everything they owned, they lost everything they had ever

Just about the only visible evidence of Kaskaskia, Illinois, was this church.

known. They no longer had neighborhoods to go back to.

The flood changed people's lives in dramatic ways. About 25,000 people in Des Moines, Iowa, were left without water when the city's water treatment plant was flooded. "We had to travel 20 miles to shower at a high school," said Tyan Smith, age seventeen. "I always took water for granted. I will never do that again."

Many children could not begin school in August as planned because their schools had vanished. In Elwood, Kansas, the Missouri River swallowed up the only elementary school, carrying off math books and kindergarten desks,

Testing the water in Des Moines

trombones and clarinets, saws and drill presses.
The gymnasium floor floated away in pieces.

Thousands of people lost their jobs. The barge
industry alone lost $2 million a day. A barge is a
large flat boat that carries goods down a river,
sometimes taking them to the ocean, where
huge ocean liners transport the goods overseas.
The Mississippi River is the central water "high-
way" for barges in the United States. Eighty
million tons of cargo are usually transported up
and down the river between St. Paul and St.
Louis. With the flood, however, barges could not

As the flood wore on, barge traffic backed up, and industries relying on the barges lost millions of dollars. Countless businesses suffered damage, such as this lumberyard in Des Moines, Iowa (inset).

navigate the treacherous Mississippi. Instead of carrying the barges, the river now carried debris—chicken coops, pianos, picnic tables, raw sewage, trees, auto parts, propane tanks, dead animals, and tons upon tons of mud.

Farmers who lived on the floodplains were hit especially hard. They watched helplessly as their crops—soy, corn, sorghum, and wheat— drowned in the water. Not only were the year's crops ruined, but three million acres of farmland went unplanted for the next season. "Normally out my front window, I see one hundred acres of corn," said Patty Nelson, of Clinton, Iowa. "Now these farm fields no longer exist. It's all water."

The worst moment of the summer for many people came after the flood was over, when the waters began to sink back into the ground. It was only then that they could see how much damage the flood had caused. Tears came to

This barn and farmhouse, normally surrounded by acres of fertile land, are in danger of being swept away in the muddy current.

Gerald McLee's eyes when he entered his house for the first time since the flood. A four-foot watermark stained the walls just like a ring around a bathtub. The floors were knee-deep in thick, slimy, brown mud. The ceilings were cracked, the carpets were rotted, and the warped floorboards had popped up. "I cried the whole first week," said Gerald's wife, Mary Jo. For months after the flood, the McLees had to live in a rented trailer in the backyard while they repaired their house.

Nine-year-old Tonya Gerdes of Elwood, Kansas, cried when she went back to the mobile

Thousands of evacuated residents returned to find their homes in a mess. Some houses simply could not be salvaged.

home where she had lived. "It's so hard to believe the river would do that to your home," Tonya said. Her new desk was smashed into pieces by the flood. "The river's just floating along as innocent as it could be, like an innocent person, like it didn't do it. You want to cry, but you can't be mad at it. It had to do it sooner or later with all that water in it."

Tonya was especially upset because the flood had ruined her baby pictures. They were lost to her forever. Considering all the flood's damage, photographs might not seem very important. But you would be surprised how many people found the loss of their photo albums to be the

Farmers not only lost acres of land, but they had to scramble to save their livestock as well.

The flood destroyed thousands of homes and businesses, but it also took an emotional toll on its victims.

most awful loss to bear. Photos capture memories; they record your own personal history. "You can take more pictures," said Becky Riddle, crying, "but you can never replace [the ones from] the Christmas of 1990."

For many of the flood victims, the experience of loss was so traumatic that they suffered long after the waters had gone down. "I shake all over. My stomach ain't right. My nerves are bad. I get a choking feeling when I eat," said Dorothy LeFever, whose town, Alexandria, Missouri, was wiped out by the flood.

For a long time, ten-year-old Rashad Bolden had the same nightmare every night. "I'm on a ladder and the water starts rising." In his dream, he tries to run from the water, but the roads all crumble around him.

The elderly perhaps suffered more than

anyone. Because of their fixed incomes and frailty, they could not rebuild their lives and homes so easily. "It will take years to get over this," said Lowell Trouillion of Cape Girardeau, Missouri. "Some never will."

Even before the floodwaters receded, questions were raised about whether people should be allowed to live on a floodplain. Some people argued that it costs too much money to rebuild everything that a flood destroys. The 1993 flood caused more than $12 billion of property and crop damage.

President Clinton surveys the damage from a helicopter.

While individual families decided whether they would stay or move out of danger, some entire towns decided to pick up and move. The 900 inhabitants of Valmeyer, Illinois, vacated their position on the floodplain and relocated on higher ground to the east. On December 3, 1993, President Bill Clinton signed a bill providing $110 million to help people in the floodplains move to higher ground. The plan entailed buying land from the residents and setting it aside for parks or wetlands.

It is not, however, so easy to force people to move, even when it's for their own good. Many people firmly believe that even though another flood may invade their lives, they should rebuild. Just weeks after the '93 floodwaters had receded, people were busy hammering new shingles on rooftops, washing walls, pulling out

torn carpets, and nailing in new floors. Vernon McClane had a smile on his face while volunteers from the Salvation Army dug up barrelfuls of sludge from his home and helped him carry out his ruined furniture, smashed television set, and mud-drenched curtains. He, like tens of thousands of others, was not going to give up. Nature would not defeat him.

Vernon McClane cleans up

The majority of flood victims did go back to their towns. But what will they do to prepare for the next flood, if there is one? Will stronger and higher levees be built? Is it worth the hundreds of millions of dollars to replace all the broken levees? In the next flood, they may just break again. As the writer Mark Twain said about the Mississippi, "[you] cannot tame that lawless stream . . . cannot say to it, Go Here or Go There, and make it obey." No levee could be built, said Twain, that the Mississippi "will not tear down, dance over and laugh at."

Some people say that levees are actually part of the problem. During a normal flood, the river overflows in many different directions at many points along a river. But when numerous levees are constructed along a river, each levee stops the flood from naturally spreading over its banks. The water gets bottled up. It rises higher and higher, and it eventually has to burst someplace. When the river does finally burst, its power is much greater than if it had been allowed to flood naturally farther upstream. During the summer of 1993, when a levee saved one town, sometimes the next town downstream was hit. "One man's levee is another man's flood," said biologist Norm Stucky.

Another difficult question raised by the flood of 1993 is whether farmers in the floodplains should be required to change their farming techniques. Farmers use chemical fertilizers and pesticides to help their crops grow. When floodwater swarms over the farmland it becomes contaminated with these chemicals. During the '93 flood, more than 12,000 pounds of atrazine (a popular weed killer) floated down the Mississippi River, perhaps poisoning the area's drinking water supply.

A farmer sprays his crops (inset). When farms are flooded (below), the chemicals in the soil can poison the local water supply.

The problems caused by the flood did not go away when the waters receded. And neither did the difficult questions about how to deal with floodplain farming and living. The answers to these questions are as murky as the Mississippi water itself.

The flood experience is not just a gloomy story. Disasters often have the strange result of bringing out the worst in nature and the best in people. There were heroes, like Ronald Vogt, who swam down a flooded street to save a fifteen-year-old. Or Denise Harshe, who swam through a basement window to rescue a man trapped in his house.

Volunteers from all over the country traveled to the flood areas and tried to help as much as they could. They worked in shelters, field

Flood victims and dedicated volunteers worked beyond the point of exhaustion to build sandbag levees.

The Salvation Army and other charitable organizations helped by providing flood victims with food, medicine, shelter, and financial assistance.

kitchens, warehouses, and house restoration units. The Salvation Army served more than one million hot meals in cafeterias set up especially for the victims. Even pets were not forgotten. The Chicago Veterinary Medical Association set up a food supply mission for lost animals, arranging to have food sent by naval air force pilots.

The Army Corp of Engineers distributed 30,000 sandbags to volunteers who piled them up at the levees. Among the volunteers were

prisoners from Farmington Correctional Center in St. Genevieve, Missouri. "We had one lady who had tears in her eyes, she was so happy to see guys from prison coming to help," said Ken Novak, one of the prisoners who lent a hand.

   Children also helped out. Rebecca Mayes, age seven, stood in front of the Baldwin Hardware store in Ironton, Missouri, and collected money. Eleven-year-old Jackie Gassel went door-to-door collecting donations in a coffee can. Three boys in Ellisville, Missouri, washed cars to earn money for their community. Amy Sheppard, age twelve, made cookies with her friends in Alton, Missouri, and sold them for ten cents a bag.

"We're too little to sandbag," she said. "We just wanted to help."

Since time began, people have had to deal with floods. Rivers are vital to villages, cities, and nations, but they can often turn into frightening enemies. In 1993, people along the Mississippi suffered through yet another battle with their river run wild. The great brown river had shown its might once again.

Yet the 1993 midwest flood is not only a story about the power of nature. After the waters receded, people began to build their lives anew. Even after a terrible disaster, there is hope.

INDEX

PHOTO CREDITS

Project Editors: Shari Joffe and Mark Friedman
Design and Electronic Composition: TJS Design
Photo Editor: Jan Izzo
Cornerstones of Freedom Logo: David Cunningham

ABOUT THE AUTHOR

Karin Luisa Badt has a Ph.D. in comparative literature from the University of Chicago and a B.A. in literature and society from Brown University. Ms. Badt has taught at the University of Rome and the University of Chicago.